MONEY -
HOW TO MAKE YOUR MONEY WORK FOR YOU

The Financial Glow Up Series

No.2

Wanda P. Bowman

Copyright © 2021 by Wanda P. Bowman
All rights reserved.

Contents

Preface v

Part I	HOW TO MAKE YOUR MONEY WORK FOR YOU
Chapter 1	Change Your Mindset 3
Chapter 2	Developing A Relationship with Money 12
Chapter 3	How to Multiply It 16
Chapter 4	Passive Income 19
Chapter 5	Royalties 21
Chapter 6	What is Drop Shipping? 23
Chapter 7	Real Estate Investing 26
Chapter 8	The Power of Making Money While You Sit At Home ... 29
Chapter 9	Wholesaling 39
Chapter 10	Lease Options 46

Part II	HOW TO MANAGE IT
Chapter 11	Avoiding Impulse Spending 55
Chapter 12	How Are You Spending the Money that You Earn? 64
Chapter 13	Plugging Spending Leaks 67

Part III	HOW TO SAVE IT AND INVEST IT
Chapter 14	Develop a Savings Plan 71
Chapter 15	Execute the Savings Plan 76
Chapter 16	Types of Savings Vehicles 79
Chapter 17	Protect Your Assets 82
Chapter 18	Dominion Over Debt 84
Chapter 19	Conclusion 86

Preface

Money is not everything, but it is an essential part of living. Beyond the basic needs, money helps us to achieve our goals and helps us to support and sustain the things that we care about (family, education, healthcare, hobbies, and leisure time).

The primary thing that money can do for you is give you freedom. This freedom allows you to decide where and how you want to live your life. It gives you freedom of choice. On the other hand, when you do not have much money, choice may be something that you cannot afford.

Some may say that money is an obsession and feel uncomfortable talking about it. They feel more comfortable talking about ways to give and sow the seed to the underserved instead of how to accumulate more of it. Well, here is what I have to say, it takes tools and resources to serve and financially impact the underserved. Yes, I agree, with the saying that the love of money could be a source of evil, but I also know this, through my years of living, the lack of money will never build hospitals, churches, or any other social institution.

I want to share with you the things that I have learned through my years of studying accounting and personal finance. I will also give you tips that I have acquired through my own personal experience and my observation of others who have obtained financial independence. I will also share some tips on how to invest in Real Estate and generate additional streams of income.

Until you are serious about having dominion over your finances, it will not register in your mind that the choices you make today will determine how comfortable you live tomorrow. I am always candid to speak about the poor choices my husband and I made in our younger years and the poor job we did in managing our finances. The things that I write in this book are learned from professional training and the "hard knocks university" of life. Therefore, I am comfortable talking about how to build wealth even after you have made poor financial decisions.

This book is a continuation of my first book "Building Your Finance Empire One Brick at a time – subtitled "The Financial Glow Up". I have lived it, breathed it, and have a t-shirt to prove it *(literally I have t-shirts called "the financial glow up")*.

Let me say this, I am attempting to address a societal need by writing this book. It is money that makes the world go around, not the lack of it. So, let us get this fact settled, we need money in order to grow the economy. I do not know about you, but I feel that it is better to be a sower than a reaper. In fact, the Bible states just that. The Bible is a great source of reference for spiritual and natural growth. In fact, that is where I learned that it is okay to be strategic and think of ways to grow your money. This is where I read, "this book of the law shall not depart out of thy mouth", because if one follows its principles it teaches how to make our way prosperous and have good success -Joshua 1:8, King James version.

Okay, now that I have laid the framework for this book let us start talking about the subject matter "Money".

What exactly is money?

Money is a tool that we use to allocate our resources. It determines how we obtain our essential wants and needs of life. It determines what economic bracket you are in and gives you the ability to affect the gross national product – which is how goods and services are produced and provided in the economy. Many who have obtained wealth have learned how to have a meaningful relationship with money.

If you become wise with your interaction with money and the accumulation of wealth you can build a financial relationship that will last your lifetime and your children's lifetime.

When we do not develop a good relationship with money, we develop a cycle of poor relationships with money that can spill over to our children.

How do you know when you do not have a good relationship with money? It is when you do not have your money working for you. If you want your money to work for you, then you should never live your life with the mindset that the only way to make money is to work in a 9:00 to 5:00 work environment. We must strategically figure out how to make our money work for us instead of us working for it.

Why do we need money?

Money makes it easier to take care of your health, your lifestyle, your family, and your legacy. It opens doors to experiences and allows you to have opportunities that the person with no money could never experience. It also allows you the ability to sow into someone else's vision and enable the economy to grow beyond your sphere of influence.

Here are some keys to building wealth:

Give your money an assignment. Put it to work. Treat your money like an employee and you the employer.

Look at every dollar that you own, present and future by percentage, and tell that dollar where it should go.

For example:

- 10% tithes and/or charity
- 10% savings/investment – long term
- 10% savings short term/emergency savings fund
- 50% needs (food clothing and shelter)
- 20% wants (miscellaneous spending)

THERE ARE THREE (3) THINGS WE NEED TO KNOW ABOUT MONEY IN ORDER TO BE FINANCIALLY INDEPENDENT

- HOW TO MAKE YOUR MONEY WORK FOR YOU

- HOW TO MANAGE YOUR MONEY

- HOW TO SAVE AND INVEST IT

PART I

HOW TO MAKE YOUR MONEY WORK FOR YOU

Chapter 1

Change your Mindset

Let us take a moment, to think about the thoughts that we have carried in our bag through the years.

Our psychological connection with money is shaped by our own family history. It is an emotional connection that moves with us through our life span.

Many of our spending habits early on were influenced by our family history, but as time evolves, our social and cultural beliefs, education and training can shift our behavior to a more positive and meaningful relationship with money.

Take a moment and close your eyes and think about some of the prevalent thoughts that have been present with you since your childhood. Now open your eyes and look at where you are currently in life.

If you are honest with yourself, you are exactly where you thought you would be.

If you thought such things as, "I will always be broke", and look at your bank account, it is exactly where you thought it would be - empty. There is extreme power in our thoughts, they control our emotions, our relationships with people and things that we possess.

What are some of the first thoughts that enter your mind, when someone says the word Money?

Many of our parents did not have the opportunity to choose a job that fit their skill set or talents. In fact, some of them did not even know what their talents were. All they knew is that they had a family to take care of and feed, so they took the first job that could give them a decent wage and comfortable life. Therefore, many of our parents worked in jobs that they did not even like but knew that if they wanted to have a reasonable lifestyle, they needed the income.

As a result, they went to work, as a necessity, not as a career path to bigger and/or better things in life.

Some of you have been taught to think about money a certain way since you were a child. You may have seen negative examples of people with money. For example, family members talking about how broke they are. Let us look at the word "broke" (which is something that we should not even use in our vocabulary). Broke means that something is not whole (Webster's definition of broke: broken, reduced to pieces or fragments). Our words have power and causes our behavior to respond in turn. You may also recall family members talking about how they could not afford to live, because their "money was funny".

As a result of these types of mindsets and psychological influences on our environment, oftentimes, when family members would get a hold of lump sums of money, they would not manage it with good judgement. Some would spend the money on non-essential wants and excessive grown-up toys without the thought of investing into something that would yield perpetual income. This often ended in them crying the blues a few months down the road when the money was gone and there was nothing of value to show for it. This mismanagement of money resulted in heart and gut-wrenching regrets. I have heard too many conversations after a big loss from mismanagement of money, about what they could have, should have and would have done with their money, if they had only known better. Some of us have had bad experiences surrounding money at some point and carry around these bad feelings our entire lives.

If you have an unhealthy relationship with money, you will never create the abundance you wish to obtain. To change your financial world, you need to change your feelings and your mindset about money. You need to change the way you think, feel and act about money.

I know this firsthand; you see I was a college graduate with a husband and a good first starter job as a staff accountant. Although, I made decent money at the time, I did not know how to strategically make my money work for me. Although, my college training prepared me for a great career path, my lack of understanding of money caused me to be reckless in managing the money that I was earning. So, although, I knew how to earn money, I had not mastered how I would spend or multiply it, and thus, I was still living paycheck to paycheck along with the rest of my peers at that time.

Many may have come from households with either a single parent or a one job father that only made enough for the rent or mortgage, utilities, and groceries. There may have been few discussions, if any at all, on savings or investing monies to create and build wealth for future generations.

I was the first generation of my family to go to college and graduate, so I had no example of wealth creation or legacy building to model my young adult life. Most of the television series on television was always about a struggling family, with lots of love but little money.

Here is what you may not have been told, your family background, your IQ, your degree, nor your social status are relevant when it comes to earning money. Many of the richest people on the planet did not finish college. In fact, many of them came from immigrant families with no wealth.

If you believe that you will never have enough money, then you will never have enough money. What you focus on the most, gives you exactly what you focus on the most. One of the most powerful quotes I have heard is "As a man thinketh, so is he".

Once we change the way we think about a thing, we change the trajectory of the relationship with that thing.

When we change how we think about ourselves and our ability to succeed, there will be a shift in our universe. Once we decide not to conform to our environment but transform our thinking by the renewing of our mind, we have positioned ourselves to transcend to a higher dimension and have established a path to greatness.

The ability to make money and accumulate it, is simply a mindset. If you understand the purpose of money and develop a meaningful relationship with it, you will be able to accumulate wealth and change the entire economic structure of your family and your legacy. The key is making the paradigm shift in your mind to allow money to become attracted to you.

Let me introduce to you Four Money Mindsets that I learned to adopt in my younger days:

Growth Mindset:

Have you heard the saying "think yourself rich, and you will become rich, think yourself poor and you will become poor"?

Now this statement is pretty much over exaggerating the concept of a mindset impact on your wealth, but there is some truth in this statement.

We must train our mind and thoughts to think of ways in which we can become wealthy and better managers of our resources. We must get into the habit of thinking that we can become wealthier. This is what is called a growth mindset. It is the idea that intelligence and skills can be developed. If you just pause for a moment and think about it, every skill or habit that you have acquired through life was learned from your environment by practicing the behavior you observed on a continual basis, whether it was intentional or non-intentional. So, what does this mean? It means that we are not limited by the environment that we were born into or the current skills or qualities that we currently possess. We have

the capability and potential to learn new habits and acq[uire]
we set our mind and energy to it.

Many of us may not have been taught about personal finance a[s]
so we must catch up to where we should be by changing our mindse[t]
towards money and the accumulation of wealth.

Now, I must admit this is not an easy habit to start because of the following:

- Money is an emotional topic. It is not easy to sit down and evaluate our wasteful spending. It is difficult to give up bad spending habits and the lifestyle that you have become accustomed to for so long. Thinking about these things can lead to feelings such as guilt or shame, and thoughts that you could have been farther ahead in life if only you had made the right choices at a younger age.
- You are also forced to plan and think ahead and eliminate impulse spending. This may also cause you to look at the people that you are hanging with that make it convenient to just spend money recklessly. Things like trying to keep up with your peers that you enjoy spending time with on vacations or weekend meetups. Some of you will have to make a full 360-degree turn, but although it may be painful in the beginning it will yield a good return in the end.

Here are a few action steps that you can start on right away.

- Identify the things that trigger you to commit emotional spending. *Sadness, Need to feel secure,*
- Once you identify those things, think of a remedy to combat it. (for example if you have a co-worker that always pushes your button in the lunchroom at lunch time, change the time that you eat lunch to avoid them; or if you have that family member that always calls you with controversial topics, stop picking up the phone and set aside a certain time that you will call them back when you are at a good space in your mind).

- Identify the negative thoughts that you think during the day that cause you to spend money to "make you feel better" and re-adjust the way you think about it. Make an intentional decision when those negative thoughts come into your mind to shift your thoughts to something pleasant that make you feel good. Now, this will not be an easy thing to accomplish in the beginning but remember the more you are intentional about eliminating negativity in your life, you will gradually see a shift in your thought patterns.

Read up on behavioral psychology. Developing an understanding of how our mind works help us more easily train it into doing what we want it to do.

Systems Based Mindset:

Our personal finances and our physical fitness are similar in a lot of ways. It takes discipline to master both. We must be intentional about what we eat and how much we exercise to be in control of our health and physical wellbeing. Well, it is the same way with our personal finances, we must be intentional and set specific goals and actions in place to be financially fit and independent in our life.

We must set SMART goals (specific, measurable, attainable, result-focused, and time-bound). The first thing we must do is to identify what we want to save for and what amount of wealth we want to accumulate. Next, we must create a list of things that we must accomplish to achieve the desired results. If the goals are lofty, then we must break them down into smaller chunks and go after the low hanging fruit first. For example, if you want to create an emergency savings fund, you must figure how much you need (i.e. three to six months of living expenses).

Next determine how much you need to save a month to build this fund and then go after it. I have found that the easiest way to save is to have it automatically deducted from my paycheck or checking account so that I will have a systematic way of saving. When you automate, it eliminates the ability to procrastinate and say you will wait until the next pay to save. The money is out of sight and out of mind. Another goal could be to pay off credit card debt. What has worked for me, is that I target the lowest balance card and start paying extra on that each month, and then when that is paid off, go after the next balance and pay what I was paying on the card that I just paid off along with the payment that is due on that one each month, and so forth and so forth. You will find that once you get into a routine of doing these things, it will become easy to maintain. Also, the joy that you feel when you have paid off one card balance is motivation enough to keep you on the journey of being debt free.

Realist Mindset:

Have you ever been at the clothing store and picked up an item, and thought to yourself, "this dress is going to make me feel better about myself when I wear it so I must purchase it", or "this pair of shoes is going to make my legs look so nice when I wear it to this special event that I have on the calendar"? Often you find that when you get the shoes home you then find that you have 4 other pairs of shoes that look just like it, but you can't take it back to the store, because it was a final sale.

This is what I call impulse buying. Being at the mall, walking around because you were bored at home and wanted to get out of the house. Unfortunately, this type of shopping; buying things just because you can, is simply just that, buying things. I have read that if you disentangle the result of what you want from what you are buying you can save yourself unnecessary spending.

Even worse, when we try to buy things just to make ourselves feel better, important, or more loved, we are just spending money that can never accomplish those things, and oftentimes we get it home and decide that we don't even want it anymore. It was just what it is called emotional spending. We are trying to change the way we feel with a material item.

So how do we critically analyze our impulse buying and embrace a realist mindset?

If you notice that your desire to buy the item(s) is a result of wanting to be a certain way, you may want to reconsider the purchase. There are other ways to getting to where you want to be that are cheaper and more sustainable.

There is nothing wrong, at times, with buying an occasional affordable luxury items – if it is affordable.

Action Items: Developing a Realist Mindset:

- When you are faced with an impulse purchase you want to buy right this second; pause, take a deep breath, and take a couple of moments to think about why you want the item. Asking yourself "WHY" five times, is a good rule-of-thumb for uncovering what really motivates you.
- Keep a spending journal. Write down how you felt about buying the item immediately after you purchased it, and then a few weeks later, write down how you feel about the purchase. If it is returnable and you have not worn it, then try to return it to the store.

Abundance Mindset:

It is so easy to look at our lives and point out areas that we are lacking, especially when we look at others and compare our life to their lifestyle or possessions.

There is always going to be someone that is richer, smarter, or prettier, but that is okay. We should not yield to the knee jerk feeling of trying to buy what someone else has so that we can feel just as important as we think they are. You do not know how much debt they are in or how much difficulty they are having to maintain that lifestyle. Even if they are not struggling to maintain that lifestyle, we should never be envious or jealous of the success of others. We must learn to appreciate the things that we have in life and learn how to be grateful for what we have and stay on the path that we need to achieve our own financial independence and personal self-fulfillment.

We should be focused on our goals and purpose and when we feel the urge to compete with someone else, just remember that we should also look inward to our skills and talents and work towards being the best version of ourselves that we can be. We should applaud our accomplishments thus far and continue to grow and learn and be uncompromising in our pursuit to achieving our goals in life.

Excerpt from "Adopt these 4 Money Mindsets and Save More" by Sarah Eadie

Money comes in, money goes out. For many people this is about as deep as their understanding gets when it comes to money and their personal finances. A few people leave their finances to chance. Each week is filled with uncertainty of what they will be able to afford or spend money on. If you ask them a question, do you think you will be able to go to this basketball game with me or go to a concert, their response will sound something like this, "I have to see how my money is looking on next week". Do you want to live your life like this? I can answer that question for you, No! You do not have to live life like this.

How do I know this? I was one of those people that had no control or understanding of where my money was going. I was living paycheck to paycheck and hoping to have extra money if I needed to purchase an item that was not rent, gas or food.

We must change our mindset about money, right at the start. We should never think that we are not good enough, or smart enough to have a meaningful relationship with earning money.

Let us do a brief exercise.

Ask yourself these questions:

What type of spending have you practiced over the last year?

Was it an impulse/emotional purchase because of feeling sad, or was it an intentional purchase that was really needed at the time you bought it?

Chapter 2

Developing a Relationship with Money

With every opportunity that we get to improve our life and earn money, we must always put our best foot forward. With each opportunity that you get to earn money, we must look at it as a new relationship with money that we are forming. Just think about it, when you are trying to impress someone you are dating, you put on your best makeup, perfume, and clothes. You dress to impress. Now if, we take this same approach to money, we will change the direction of our financial path to one of economic growth and financial independence. We must be focused on what we need to accomplish.

With this focus we must become consistent and persistent in understanding the purpose of making our money work for us. This is more important than willpower, because when you are focused you never take your eye off the prize.

We were created to be fruitful, by multiplying our wealth and having dominion over the things that we work for. Our accumulation of wealth is not just for us but it is to be a positive influence on others. Once we realize that we have the power to be prosperous we will do the things that will bring us closer to our purpose. This takes focus and perseverance. All it takes is to reverse our negative thinking to productive thinking. Our mind will then be able to channel our thoughts in a positive direction.

The problem with us is that we are too busy focusing on what other people think about us that we take our eyes off the prize.

A wise woman once told me not to focus my thoughts on other people's opinions about me, because their opinions are none of my business.

You need to know your assignment, your purpose in life and build your daily tasks around them. If what you are doing does not fit into your purpose or the plan that has been designed for you, do not give it the time of day. The enemies of your success (which are fear, doubt, and unbelief) will use negative experiences and people to taunt you with unnecessary drama to get you off your game plan. Do not take the bait, stay focused.

Do not listen to the voices that give you reasons why you should not or cannot accomplish your goals.

Do not listen to the dream snatchers, the vision killers, or the destiny assassins.

Listen to the voices that give you the reasons why you can and will achieve the goals that you set.

Do not let anyone define your ability and capability through their narrow lens of criticism, but it is time for you to build your own dream.

I quote Bruce Lee – "The successful warrior is the average man, with laser-like focus".

These are five things that I have discovered on my journey to financial independence:

- If you believe you will never have enough money, you will never have enough money. What you focus and think on the most responds accordingly. You are what you think!
- If you really believe that abundance is available to all, you will end up attracting your own abundance.
- If you do not pay attention to your money, you will have no idea where it is going. If you want your relationship with money to

improve you must pay it some attention. Think of it as a marriage. Stop ignoring it and start appreciating it.
- Stop waiting for someone to make you rich! God has given to everyone the tools they need to prosper and get wealth. Everything that you need to get wealth is intrinsic. It is all contained in your mind and determination to achieve the goals that you set for yourself. You must tap into your purpose.
- No one is going to make you rich. No one is going to discover you or fix you. You must put the hard work in and know that you are deserving of success.

Money is only a tool. If used properly, it can build a financial empire that will enable you to be a blessing to the world.

There is a unique relationship with money that wealthy people have mastered. They have developed the innate ability to attract opportunities that generate money. To become financially independent, we must develop that ability. Instead of us always chasing the dollar, we should live a life that money is attracted to us. We become the magnet that draws money to us. Instead of us pursuing it, it pursues us.

It is not how much money you make, but how much money you can keep, how hard it works for you and how much you can hand off to generations to come.

Despite how it may appear, having strong financial values does not necessarily mean being wealthy or even having a lot of financial knowledge. A person with truly little money can still be driven by financial values.

There are three values that one must possess to maintain financial independence:

- Accuracy – be precise as to what you want to accomplish
- Organization – develop a plan with measurable action steps
- Discipline – be committed to staying with the plan and execute with extreme focus and develop a maintenance plan to protect what you have achieved

Once you know what you want and stay focused on the plan it will ultimately lead to your achievement of that goal. This mindset applied to your skillset and money-making ability will inevitably increase your earning potential.

These skills are essential in learning how to make your money work for you.

How you make your money is up to your imagination and your skill set. Could you pick up a side project or a second job? Could you make more money in your current job by gaining new skills, or could you get a better paying job by going back to school?

Chapter 3

How to Multiply It

The only fulfilling way that I know to earn money, is by doing what you love. I am not saying that you cannot earn money by not doing what you love, but I am saying the most fulfilling way to earn it is by doing something you are passionate about.

We talked about the importance of your mindset in Chapter 1. Many people end up poor because of the mindset and thoughts that they have carried all of their life. The circumstances of having no money often spill into the psychology of being poor. When you cannot see yourself breaking out of poverty you become stuck in that state. You can be broke, but you never want to be poor.

When you have a poor person's mindset, you are creating a psychological barrier that keeps you from getting money because you just don't expect to get any. (excerpt from "The Mindset You Must Adopt to Make More Money by Ayodeji Awosika)

It is critical that for you to be placed in a position to generate additional streams of revenue beyond your 9 to 5 job you must have a mindset shift that is crucial to your ability to attract money making ventures.

You consume, buy, and take on many expenses that you pay to other people or corporations, but you yourself only produce value from one source your day job.

The question many Americans face is how secure is their job in times of economic downturns? How many jobs have been loss due to freak occurrences? Displaced people cannot get up and learn a new skill overnight. It takes sometimes years to develop and learn a new skill to generate a new income.

Lessons learned from the many economic crisis's that we have experienced over the last decade is that there is no such thing as job security, therefore we must position ourselves to be able to have more than one source of revenue flowing in our households.

We have been taught to make money through the narrowest lens of life. We have been told to go to college and choose a career that is compatible to our skill set. We have been told to build our economic future around this one source of income. When you have one source of income from an employer, and you do this for years, you come to think of this as the only possible way to make money. You see advertisements on the internet about generating additional streams of money, but you do not believe it

Don't get me wrong, there are some scams out there, but there also are legitimate ways of making money that can generate multiple streams of income that will allow you to become financially independent and live a comfortable life now and in the future.

We must look for other ways to generate revenue that is compatible with our passions. The thing that stops most people from stepping outside of the box and seeking other business opportunities is the negative feedback we get from our friends or family members. To combat the negative feedback, you may receive from others you must surround yourself with like-minded people that can help you get to your next level of generating additional revenue streams.

A lot of times we hang on to unnecessary baggage and relationships that are anti-purpose. We need to know the difference between people that are "dream builders" and those that are "dream killers". We must also discover our true passion and purpose in life and perfect that skill.

That is why it is so important to know your purpose in life and to be cognizant of the resources and relationships you will need that will be instrumental in helping you achieve the milestones to your next level of financial freedom. Let us be clear about the fact that every one's definition of financial freedom is different. Some people may not want a big mansion on the hill, they are content with the quaint little home with the picket white fence. Again, all that matters is that you are living the lifestyle that you desire without worrying about maintaining and sustaining that level of economic independence.

Once you find things that you love, then we can focus on how to successfully earn money.

You must make the switch from being a consumer of goods to a producer of goods and understand that there is some segment of the market that can use your services. Based on your current skill set or the ones that you are developing you can tap into a market that can generate additional streams of revenue.

There are so many business models out there to choose from to generate additional revenue streams.

In the next few chapters I am going to share some of the revenue streams that my husband and I have tapped into that have helped us to generate additional revenue streams.

Chapter 4

Passive Income

As I mentioned earlier in the book, your earned income is going to be your biggest source of generating wealth, but we all dream of ways to make additional income.

As discussed earlier, due to the volatility of economic downturns and uncertainty of job security it is always good to have additional streams of income beyond your day job.

Passive income can be a great supplementary source of funds for many people, and it can prove to be an especially valuable lifeline during a recession or during other tough times, such as the government lockdown imposed in response to the coronavirus pandemic. Passive income can keep money flowing when you lose a job or otherwise experience some financial hardship.

If you are worried about being able to save enough of your earnings to meet your retirement goals, building wealth through passive income is a strategy that might appeal to you.

What exactly is passive income?

Passive income is income that requires little to no effort to earn and maintain. It is called progressive passive income when the earner expends little effort to grow the income. Examples of passive income include rental income and any business activities in which the earner does not materially participate.

Some of the top methods of passive income that I have seen are described below:

- Royalties
- Online business/drop-shipping
- Real Estate investments
- Investing

Royalties – an example of royalties are music royalties – compensatory payment received by rights holders (songwriters, composers, recording artists, and their respective representative) in exchange for the licensed use of their music. (Soundcharts team published January 8, 2020)

Online Drop-shipping is a type of retail fulfillment method. Business owners do not have to carry inventory. Purchases are made from a third-party supplier.

Real Estate is often considered one of the biggest passive money makers. The pitch sounds reasonable enough - put your money into buying rental units (houses or apartments), and you can get paid every month by the renters. Money is constantly rolling in, and you do not have to lift a finger, or you can buy properties to resale to other consumers.

Investing in real estate for passive income is not one size fits all. Before wading in, first figure out which investment strategy works best for you.

Chapter 5

Royalties

Music Royalties

There are two types of music rights: Master vs. Composition

Master: the copyright for the composition. It is created when the composition is turned into a sound recording and owned by recording artists and their record labels.

Composition: songwriters and their music publishers own the copyright for the harmony, melody, and lyrics. Composition copyright is when your musical work is committed to a notepad, sheet music, or even a tweet.

How do Royalties work?

- Artists create
- Artists or agent contact the intermediaries (mediums that pay out royalties.)
- Music is played
- Intermediaries tracks music, collects, and distributes royalties.
- Rights holders are paid

There are six (6) different types of royalties:

- Streaming royalties
- Neighboring royalties

- Digital performance royalties
- Sync licensing fees
- Public performance royalties
- Mechanical royalties

Who gets paid when the royalties are distributed?

Today, the bulk of mechanical royalties are generated by digital streaming platforms (dsp). Any time a user chooses to play a specific song on demand – the streaming service pays out the mechanicals.

There are many different parties with fingers in the pot, some rights holders get the monies paid directly to them and some go through a middleman. As you can imagine, the middleman gets a percentage, thus cutting into the amount of the money the rights holder receives.

Here is a high level of parties that get paid royalties:

- Recording artists
- Record labels
- Distributors
- Licensing companies
- Songwriters
- Publishers

The above are very high-level definitions of how royalties are created and generated. This book is just an introduction to how artists and music makers can generate additional streams of revenue by creating good product and understanding the music business while having someone effectively manage and monitor their work and the products they create.

Chapter 6

What is Drop Shipping?

Simply put, drop-shipping is a streamlined form of business wherein the seller accepts customer's orders but does not keep goods in stock (definition from Wikipedia).

Drop-shipping is a type of business model which enables a company to operate without maintaining inventory, owning a warehouse to store their products, or even having to ship their products to their customers themselves. How it works is that the retailer partners with a dropship supplier that manufactures and/or warehouses products, packages the products, and ships them directly to the retailer's customer, on the retailer's behalf.

In simpler terms, this is how drop-shipping works:

- The customer places an order for a product on the retailer's online store.
- The retailer automatically or manually forwards the order and customer details to the dropship supplier
- The dropship supplier packages and ships the order directly to the customer in the retailer's name.

This type of business is extremely popular for new entrepreneurs especially millennials and generation z's due to their internet and computer skills far outweighing their financial capacity. Since you do not need to stock or handle the items you are selling; it is possible to start a drop-shipping business with limited funds.

The merchant does not have to order inventory or fulfill the orders in any way. Instead, the third-party supplier takes care of the product itself.

Drop shipping is great for entrepreneurs because it does not demand as much as the traditional retail model. You do not have to open a brick-and-mortar store, pay overhead, or stock products. Instead, you open an online storefront and buy wholesale from suppliers who already have products and warehouse space.

The merchant is mainly responsible for gaining customers and processing orders in drop shipping, meaning you will effectively be a middleman. Despite this, you will reap the lion's share of the profit by marking up the items you sell. It is a simple business model and one that can be rewarding.

With drop shipping, you can build a business that is sustainable in the long term right from your laptop.

Of course, there are many drawbacks and advantages, and it is important that you look at them before you start your own drop shipping ecommerce business. Once you understand the pros and cons of drop shipping, however, learning how to do so effectively can be achieved.

Don't get me wrong learning how to start a drop shipping business, as with any type of venture, is not easy. Nevertheless, it is a great first step into the world of entrepreneurship. You can sell to customers without holding any inventory. You do not need to pay for products upfront. And if you are serious about your new venture, you can build a sustainable source of income in the long run.

If you are contemplating drop shipping, consider taking tutorials on the business and the financial steps you need to take.

Understanding the market that you are interested in pursuing for your business model is very essential. You need to do the research of the goods that you are selling and the market that you are targeting. You also should stay in touch with the trends in the industry you are entering and the competition.

In summary, if you are ready to start a business that can compete against retail giants on a limited budget then below are six steps that are essential to your success:

1. Select a niche – choose something that you are interested in and focus on what is appealing to your target audience.
2. Perform competitive research and look for products that are high in demand. Doing this will help your business model to be sustainable and remain relevant to consumers.
3. Secure a supplier – pick the right supplier because partnering with the wrong business supplier can be disastrous. Most suppliers are located overseas so make sure that you pick one with great communication skills and response time to your questions and/or concerns.
4. Build your ecommerce website. You can use simple ecommerce platform such as Shopify. Do your own research to find what best fits your business model.
5. Create a customer acquisition plan. Without customers you cannot generate sales. Start a marketing campaign (you can use such platforms as Facebook and Instagram).
6. Analyze and optimize - You need to be able to track all the data and metrics there are to grow your business (this includes google analytics traffic and other social media forums)

In summary, as with any investment that you are considering, do your own homework to determine if this is something that you want to commit your time and energy into.

Chapter 7

Real Estate Investing

Investing in Real Estate for passive income is not one-size-fits-all. Before wading in, first figure out what investment strategy works best for you.

Diversification matters as much as location.

When using Real Estate for passive income, it is important to consider the level of diversification in your portfolio. Investing in a portfolio that is diversified by property type, tenant mix and geography will greatly increase the probability that it will provide a stable and predictable stream of income over the long term. Depending on how much time and money you have available to invest in passive Real Estate, owning multiple rental properties can be profitable.

For example, consider whether you are more interested in owning an apartment building or multifamily home to generate Real Estate passive income versus a commercial building in which you are dealing with business tenants. Also think about how involved you want to be when it comes to things like collecting rent or handling repairs, and whether you would prefer to hand off those duties to a property management company.

The primary objective is to create streams of income on a recurring basis.

To be effective in this type of revenue generation you must do your homework.

You must be proactive in thoroughly researching potential investment properties. This means asking questions about the property and the seller before committing to the purchase. And if the answers you get leave you with even more questions, you should probably move on.

When my husband and I first became involved with buying rental properties, we spent a tremendous about of time doing our research.

Our first investment was buying two properties land contract which introduced us to the many benefits of rental income as a source of passive income.

This led us to increasing our purchases of properties for rental income as perpetual income.

We started exploring opportunities with governmental auctions and quickly increased our portfolio of properties.

The key to our success was the days and weeks we spent researching the properties listed in the government data bases.

We would search by zip codes and narrow our search to the areas that we thought had potential for economic growth.

We drove by the properties and looked at the outside of the home and if possible, would go into the homes to look at the infrastructure. Some auctions do not allow you to go into the home if it is being auctioned for property taxes owed only.

It is important to also drive around the neighborhood to see if there are a lot of vacant or abandoned homes. This could indicate that the area is deteriorating, and the home values are depreciating.

You must do your research and make investment decisions based on all the facts that you gather.

Obtaining the funds to purchase investment properties is not as difficult as you may think.

When buying Real Estate for passive income, taking out a loan is an obvious choice, but do not overlook the benefits of leveraging retirement assets to create rental income. A self-directed Individual Retirement Account (IRA) gives you the opportunity to make investment decisions. You can use a self-directed IRA to purchase residential rental properties, commercial rentals or even land to generate passive income. Leveraging IRA assets can help you avoid taking on debt and having interest payments on a loan detract from your returns. There are certain IRS rules to follow when taking this route, talk to a financial advisor to see which option is best for you to obtain the capital you need for your investment.

The next chapters will go into more detail about investment properties:

- Rental properties
- Wholesale properties
- Lease Options

Chapter 8

The Power of Making Money While You Sit at Home

Investing in real estate to build wealth is generally much different from buying a home to live in yourself. From the process of financing and buying a property to maintaining it, being a landlord is a job.

Here are a few things you should know:

1. Investors face more stringent lending requirements than homeowners.

    - Make sure you have a good credit score
    - Most times you must put down more than the typical 20%
    - Your debt-to-income ratio is often scrutinized more intensely
    - Oftentimes, banks require an emergency fund or cash reserves in place

2. It is a business not a home.

    - Develop your customer service skills to deal with tenants
    - Use a professional screening criterion for all tenants

3. Do not get overly emotional about your properties

    o Do not become attached to anything in the building
    o Keep your emotions out of it when dealing with difficult tenants

Real Estate has produced many of the world's wealthiest people, so there are plenty of reasons to consider this as an investment into your financial independence. But before you delve into this form of investment, you need to understand the game.

If you are going to do Real Estate, it needs to be done as a properly structured business. This will protect your personal assets from the business profits and losses associated with owning investment properties. It will also protect your personal assets should someone sue you as the owner of investment Real Estate property.

If you hold your properties under the ownership of a limited liability corporation (LLC), the business and its assets may be liable, but your personal asset should not be.

The profits from the rental properties can flow to you as an owner, but the liabilities will remain with the corporation.

Even though investing in rental properties is considered perpetual income, earning money while you sleep, it is still a hands-on investment.

It is particularly important that you invest in a location that is best suited for your investment strategy. Where you end up investing will depend largely on your personal investment goals.

If you are looking for equity growth and cash flow, there are four (4) things that you might want to take into consideration when locating properties:

- Job growth
- Population growth

- Affordability
- Familiarity with neighborhoods

Detroit, Michigan, and its metropolitan communities are some of the areas that my husband and I have invested in. One of the reasons is because we live in the area and are familiar with the surrounding Cities.

The Detroit metropolitan area has been home to several Fortune 500 companies, including Quicken Loads, Kellogg, Penske Automotive, Walmart and many more which has resulted in an increased demand in homes for rent or purchase.

Despite, Detroit's long-standing name as the automobile capital of the world, several of Detroit's fastest growing industries are in sectors as diverse as healthcare, defense, aerospace, Information Technology (IT) and logistics.

When my husband and I first started investing in rental properties, we found that the Wayne County auctions, and other auction sites were some of the best ways to get good properties at low prices.

We also learned the importance of establishing relationships with realtors to get access to new listings of properties that were in good neighborhoods. There was also a huge demand from families that wanted nice homes but could not qualify for mortgages at the time. In forming these relationships, we found out that the easiest homes to rent were the three (3) bedroom homes. We have found that even if you are renting to a couple with no children, most likely when they start a family they are going to want separate bedrooms for their children. In knowing these facts all of the homes that we targeted were 3-bedroom properties.

We looked for 3-bedroom properties that were in good neighborhoods that would also qualify for Section 8 properties, just in case we had potential customers that were getting funding from governmental sources.

So, we looked for homes that attracted median income families along with individuals that qualified for government vouchers.

At the time of writing this book here are some of the statistics that I researched about the Detroit metropolitan market:

- Metro Population: 4.3 M
- Median Household Income: $26,000
- Current Median Home Price: $190,000
- Median Rent Per Month: $1,405
- 1 Year Job Growth Rate: .76%
- 6 Year Equity Growth Rate: 69.0%
- 7 Year Population Growth: .50%
- Unemployment Rate: 5%

Data Sources:

- Zillow.com
- Factfinder.census.gov
- Deptofnumbers.com

How to find Investment Rental Properties

Things to consider in finding good properties:

- Vacancy % of areas – (is the property in an area that people are leaving because of crime or bad schools)
- Invest in areas that you are familiar
- Look at the prices of sales of homes in a 2-mile radius to determine if the property values are appreciating in the area in case you want to lease it out to tenants with the option for them to buy after a specified period.
- In general, single family homes, and condominiums are good investment properties.
    - Condos are low maintenance, because the association takes care of external repairs (disadvantages are if there is a high monthly association fee because you must build this fee into the rental payments of the tenants).

- Amenities – tour the neighborhood, and check out parks, nearby restaurants, movie, theaters, public transportation, banks, etc.
- Research types of renters that you can attract in the area you are looking to purchase rental homes
- Investing in turnkey Real Estate – it would be awesome to invest in properties that already have renters in them
- Avoid fixer uppers if you are new to the rental property business. Instead, look to buy a home that is priced below the market and needs only minor repairs.
- Are there a lot of distressed homes in the area? – Most renters do not want to live in an area that has run-down looking homes.
- If your criteria are properties that appreciate, you want to look for properties that need only a few cosmetic changes and little renovations. This will attract tenants that are willing to pay higher rental payments. This will also raise the value of your property if you expect to sell after holding for a few years.
- Estimate your rental earnings – make sure that you are making enough money from rent to cover all your costs associated with the property (i.e., mortgage, repairs, insurance, and property taxes)
- If you must obtain a mortgage what is your capitalization rate – what is the amount of time it will take you to recoup your investment.
    o If you invest $100,000 in a property and earn $5,000 per year after expenses, it amounts to a 5% cap rate. It will take you 20 years to recoup your investment.

In closing, make sure that holding rental properties is the right thing for you.

If you are not a handy man, connect with someone that knows about restoring properties. This is key to have this experience or resource at your fingertips. You do not want to own rental property and not have the capability to maintain or improve its condition. The primary reason for buying rental property, besides the ability of earning perpetual income while you sleep, is to have the property appreciate so that you can make money once you sell it.

You must have good Renters to be successful in the business.

There is nothing that can negatively affect the return on your investment like a "bad tenant".

Properly and thoroughly interviewing and screening potential tenants is vital to making sure your first rental property is a success.

You can work with a property management company if you do not have the time to vet all your renter applicants or the time to answer calls at 2:00 am in the morning about a furnace that stopped running or other company furnished appliance malfunctions.

There is no excuse not to vet "all rental applicants" when there are companies like MyRental that offer free online applications for tenants and monthly subscriptions for landlords to verify previous addresses, criminal background checks and eviction history.

Screen all prospective tenants on the phone before you agree to meet with them. This is a must, make sure you have a completed application, and they pass all of your criteria.

Do not give them a key to the property until the lease is completely executed, which clearly states who can occupy the property and the security deposit is collected.

Set up online or direct deposit rental payments, this eliminates the issue of "the check or money order got lost in the mail". With online payments, there are no excuses. Your tenants can pay you instantly with the click of the button.

For those tenants that are not technically savvy, create a Post Office box or remote location for rents to be mailed. Never let your tenants know your personal home address. Any personal information about you should not be shared with the tenants. Remember this is a business not a social networking relationship.

Below are some non-negotiable things to consider:

- Do not let a tenant move in until all repairs are completed, and you get a signed Move-in-Inspection Report from the tenant.
- Have a standard rental/lease agreement for all tenants. Check with a lawyer to make sure that all language in the contract is legal. Treat every tenant the same, it is the law.
- Inspect all your rental properties, at least quarterly, to ensure that the tenants are not damaging your properties. Do not wait until you must evict them for non-payment and find that they have damaged your property.
- Guarantee that all reported repairs are completed timely (preferably within three days of the notification). This will keep your tenants satisfied with your customer service and will help you to retain good tenants. The longer the retention of good tenants reduces the cost it takes to get the home ready for new tenants.
- Keep your rental income separate from your personal checking account. For tax purposes you should set up a separate banking account for your rental business. Do not commingle funds. This will eliminate issues with the IRS if your rental business is audited.
- Make sure that you have a good repair and maintenance team in place and a part of your team. This guarantees the credibility of service that you can receive from your maintenance team. It also ensures consistency of cost of repairs because you are using the same team for each repair job.
- Do not let your tenants randomly have repairs done without your approval of the job and vendor. This allows you to control costs of repairs and the frequency of repairs done on your property. Remember that you are the owner of the property, not the tenant.

Section 8 Property Renters

Some landlords have concerns about renting to Section 8 Housing tenants. They worry that these tenants will destroy their property and keep quality tenants from renting from them. Also, many landlords have heard horror stories about the numerous Section 8 inspections that are required of your property, when you have Section 8 tenants.

While there can be negatives when dealing with Section 8, which is referred to as the Housing Choice Voucher Program, there are many advantages as well.

My husband and I have had very few good clients that were Section 8. Some of our best tenants have been part of the Housing Choice Voucher Programs. We have one tenant that we have had for over 15 years, in fact, she has found homes for us to buy for her friends that were on Section 8 that were excellent homes.

One thing that I want to say is that when you have great quality homes for rent, the word of mouth from your tenants, will attract potential renters faster than an advertisement in the paper. Keep all properties maintained at the highest level. Your standard should be to keep them in a living condition that you would want to live in.

There are other advantages of Section 8. You can continue to collect rent even if you are going through the eviction process. This is not the case for non-section-8 tenants. For example, with non-section 8 clients that you take to court for non-payment of rent, the possibility of future rental payments during the court process is difficult to collect. Oftentimes, the moment they get an eviction notice and court date, they stopped paying rent,

But for Section 8 tenants, when you set a court date, to evict them, you will still get rent from them until the court date. Also, if they damage your property, while they are waiting to be evicting, they will lose their voucher for a future housing site.

Below are four (4) advantages of renting to Section 8 tenants:

- **Consistent rent payments from the Government**
    - Tenants have a specified pre-approved voucher for rent
    - Tenants that apply already know what they can afford

- o All rental payments are paid directly to you, so the tenant can never use their rent money for anything other than rent.
- o Tenants must be on good behavior, or they will lose their voucher

- **Targeted Marketing**
  - o Section 8 has their own website that is dedicated specifically to Section 8 tenants.
  - o Once you register on the Section 8 website, you can post any property listing that qualifies for their tenants.
  - o You also can post your listing on such sites as Craigslist, Trulia, etc.
  - o You can post in the public library, and grocery stores for those tenants that do not have technology at their fingertips.

- **Consistent Tenant Base**
  - o Another advantage is that you are opening your property to a previously untapped tenant base.
  - o There is an abundance of Section 8 tenants, so when one tenant leave your property, you will not have to keep it vacant long.
  - o If you have had a recent inspection from your previous tenant, you do not have to go through another inspection for your new tenant to move in right away.

- **Pre-screened tenants**
  - o You do not have to pre-screen your prospective tenants; Section 8 has a stringent criterion already in place to qualify your tenants
  - o All criminal background checks are done by the government before the tenant can qualify for the housing voucher
  - o All information about the previous landlords of the tenant is available to you upon request from the Government.

In conclusion, not only are your rental payments guaranteed despite the hardship conditions the tenant may fall upon, The Department of Housing and Urban Development (HUD) is known to be the best in town when it comes to rental rates. Often, you can get just as much rent in lower income neighborhoods that you can get in higher-end areas.

While it may not be for every landlord, Section 8 housing offers great benefits to landlords with one or more low-to middle-priced rental properties.

Overall, in my opinion, the benefits outweigh the disadvantages, particularly when you consider the fact that rental income checks will always show up on time.

Chapter 9

Wholesaling

What is Real Estate wholesaling? This is where a wholesaler contracts a home with a seller, then finds an interested party to buy it. As a wholesaler, you are simply the middleman. The wholesaler contracts the home with a buyer at a higher price than with the seller and keeps the difference as profit. Real Estate wholesalers generally find and contract distressed properties. The wholesaler has no intention of fixing the property, their role is simply to connect interested buyers with interested sellers.

Wholesaling of Real Estate is one of the best ways to break into the Real Estate investing industry. You do not need large sums of money for this type of investing. All you need is a good business mind, and solid work ethics. There is no age cap on this type of work, you can be anywhere from 18 to 102 and be equally successful at any age. There is no time limit or term on this type of business, you can do it until you no longer want to. There is no gender exclusivity attached to this business. There are several men and women that have found success in wholesaling. This is a good business for women that want to make extra money and can partner with people that know how to assess the condition of the home. There have been many single women that have made a nice sum of money in this industry.

In fact, Real Estate wholesaling has become synonymous with today's greatest entry level business strategies. Due, in large part, to its relatively risk adverse nature, most entrepreneurs will use wholesaling Real Estate strategies as a steppingstone towards more complex Real Estate investments. (Source: How to start Wholesaling, Fortune Builders.com)

Wholesaling of distressed properties:

Distressed Property – a distressed property is usually a result of a homeowner that is unable to keep up with the mortgage payments and/or taxes for the property. It could also be a house that has no mortgage, but the homeowner is not willing to maintain its aesthetics or property, therefore it has fallen into the category of a "ugly home" and no individual that is looking for a home to live in is willing to buy this property.

Wholesaling Concept:

The beauty of this whole concept is that you do not need to be a Real Estate agent to wholesale a piece of property. You do not have to incur all the costs or time it takes for studying associated with being a Real Estate agent. Why is this? This is because you are not actually selling the property, but you are selling the rights to purchase the property.

This concept involves reaching out to distressed sellers:

- o Seller inherited the property and does not want to maintain it
- o Seller is ill and is not able to keep the property or maintain its upkeep
- o Seller cannot sell it or find appropriate renters

These next 4 Steps are crucial:

Step 1 - Marketing:

You need to market to find deals. You must find the right kind of property to be successful. There must be enough meat on the bone to entice an investor to buy the property from you. For you to make a profit you must find deals at a low enough price point that makes sense for everyone.

How do you find these types of properties?

- Subscribe to various websites that will allow you to find vacant and/or distressed properties
- Drive through certain neighborhoods and do a mass mailing at targets addresses that fit your profile
- Social gatherings that seniors frequent – post posters up saying that you will buy homes for cash within 30 – 60 days

In these types of scenarios, it is not likely a situation where they want to maintain the property for a continued period. They are looking to unload this property if the ideal opportunity presents itself.

These will be properties that are not maintained, most of them will be vacant or soon to be vacant, due to the inability of the owner to maintain the taxes and upkeep associated with this particular property.

Things You Do:

Once you find the owner of this type of property you can have dialogue with them about the sale of their property.

Do your research. Go on Zillow to find out what this house is valued at. Then do a search within a 1 – 2-mile radius to see which homes have recently sold and what were the asking prices and selling prices.

Next do a title search on the property to determine if there are any liens on the property and if there are back taxes due on this property (you do not want to go into a deal where there are surprises at closing that you did not anticipate). This will cut into your profit margin or result in you taking a loss because you did not have all the facts before you went in a contractual relationship with the seller.

The key is – It does not matter how much you read about investments of rental properties; the onus is on you to do your own research. No one is going to be responsible for your business deal going badly. (Remember that things that are written in this book are based on actual case studies, but results may vary from individual to individual).

Step 2 – Convert Leads to Deals:

It is important to be able to convert opportunities that come your way through marketing or word of mouth into deals. Getting leads and being introduced to homeowners is great, but you need to be able to convert that conversation into a deal. Before you have that conversation with that homeowner, you need to do research on how to talk to that homeowner in a way that will stir up interest.

You need to be able to say the right buzz words that will make them feel that all their worries and stressors are about to be eliminated. You need to make them feel that you are their "Knight in Shining Armor" coming to save the day. If they are in real distress, they will be ready to sell to the one with the best sales pitch of the day. How you approach them, talk to them, and answer their questions and deal with their problems makes all the difference in the world. It may seem difficult at first when you approach your first potential deal, but once you close a deal or two, it will become easier to do. If you are not very confidant on your first deal, it may be beneficial to take along someone that is very confidant and can represent your best interest.

After you figure out your routine and get your sales pitch polished it will become routine. Remember the key is to convince them that this is the best thing that they can do with this distressed property and you must honestly feel that way. Always operate within the spirit of integrity. You never want to do something that will cause harm to the individual that you represent on the sale or that you are selling to.

Step 3 – Know your Numbers

Once you are ready to proceed with a business arrangement with the seller you can start your negotiations and necessary paperwork in process.

Offer a highly discounted price for the property, approximately 70% of market value.

Do a walkthrough of the property and estimate a cost of repairs. (Here is where it comes in handy to have a spouse, family member, or close friend that knows home repairs). If you do not have that kind of resource readily available, you can go to home improvement businesses and find them there. You can advertise that you are looking for this expertise and have someone on board within days.

Your next step is to draw up a contract with language clearly written that says that you have the right to assign the contract to a cash buyer.

Next, calculate how much you want for all the work that you have committed to this project. Remember that your time is valuable, and time is money. This fee is an assignment fee.

Below is an example of what this looks like.

The market price of this particular property is $80,000 (this is from your research). Let us say that you are offering them 70% of this price less the estimated cost of repairs for this property.

$80,000 x 70% = $56,000

Upon the walk through of the property, both inside and outside, you determine that it will take $10,000 to bring this house up to code. Remember that before any house can be sold, it must pass City inspection.

$56,000 - $10,000 = $46,000

Remember to include your desired profit into your offer. In this example, let us say you want to make $8,000 on this deal. Therefore your complete offer to the seller will be $46,000 - $8,000 = $38,000 less any liens owed on the property

Take pictures of the property – make sure you have a quality camera. You want to make sure that you have high resolution pictures to have available on your website and to show potential cash buyers in person. You do not ever want to say, I have to get back to you when a potential buyer asks to see your property. Have all your information available at the first opportunity you have to sale. Be always ready to present your best foot forward. You may not get a second chance to present. Your potential cash buyer may have moved on to the next potential wholesaler.

Also have all your forms/contracts ready for review and signature. You can hire a personal lawyer or go to Legal shield and sign up for their services to be able to use their templates for contracts. Have contracts already prepared for every type of agreement you want to enter. You want to make sure that the contract you draw up with the distressed seller has the language included that you can assign the property to a cash buyer.

Step 4 - Networking

Now the next step is to find a cash buyer. Where do you find cash buyers?

Some of the best contacts are through word of mouth from family members, friends, and co-workers. Also meeting and networking sites throughout your State. You find them at Real Estate Investor meetings, in advertisements in your local paper, social media sites and even on the internet. Some of the best contacts you will make will often come from informal settings (i.e., field trips with school events, church gatherings, holiday events and parties).

Remember what you put into your research and your hunt for the treasure is what you will get out of it. You cannot wait passively for something to fall out of the sky or be handed to you on a silver platter. You must put the work in. Do your own research!!!!!

Real example: At a local investor meeting, a family member, stood up and announced that they had a piece of property to sell for cash, with a contract already in place with the owner. Immediately at break time she was approached by an interested cash buyer. You must be ready with all the information at the time you are approached. You cannot be humming around; you need to have a contract in place. Not only was a deal struck at the 10-minute break period, but earnest money deposit was exchanged within a day or two of that conversation. Listen this is an important point (never strike a deal without that cash buyer giving you an earnest money down payment – this shows the seriousness of the intent). Do not take a personal check, take a certified check or cash). Draw up the contract.

Put language in all contracts, <u>earnest money deposit on file with a title company</u>.

Summary:

Wholesaling is a good first start into Real Estate investing. It takes very little capital to start and it is practically risk averse. Before you delve into this type of investment, always do your homework first. Understand the market in which you want to invest, build up your networking platform. You can do this by joining investment groups, subscribe to websites and local publications that deal with the sale and purchase of Real Estate.

By researching the market and building a strong buyer's list you will have a better chance at being successful. Once you have that strong buyer's list, they will become repeat customers, especially if you develop a proven track record for bringing them good properties. The best part about wholesaling that if you master this, it can be a jump start of you getting into the Real Estate investment arena.

Chapter 10

Lease Options

Another viable option for Real Estate investments is Lease Options.

In Real Estate the lease-option is a legal instrument between the investor/seller and a tenant/buyer. It involves a lease with a monthly rental amount due, but it also includes an option to buy – for a pre-determined price – at any time during the agreement. Typically, lease-options include a rental credit that goes toward the purchase of the home.

Advantages of the tenant/buyer:

- The ability to live in a nice home without stressing about qualifying at the front end for a mortgage. Having the luxury of time to get their credit in repair without losing the opportunity of living in a great home.
- Portion of rental payment goes towards the purchase price. If the tenant-buyer pays the rental amount due each month, a portion of the rental payment could go towards the purchase price should the tenant/buyer exercise their right to purchase the property. So, a portion of their rental payment will go towards the down payment of the purchase price of the home. (this is something they cannot get from renting a high-end apartment)

Advantages to the Seller:

- Seller can charge higher monthly rent (since the tenant-buyer will be occupying the home as a renter for 12 – 18 months, the seller

will miss out on the immediate financial benefits of selling the home on the market now. By charging a slightly higher rent to the tenant-buyer, the seller offsets his/her opportunity cost).
- Greater tenant responsibility – since the tenant-buyer knows that he has the option to own the home, he will take better care of the property.
- On time rental payments - in the lease to buy option, you can put language that the offer to purchase the home in the future is based on timely monthly rental payments each month. If the payments are not timely, you will forfeit the opportunity to purchase home.
- Pre-established selling price - the tenant-buyer signs a lease with an agreed upon purchase price of the home. Based on anticipated appreciation of the home, the seller can place a selling price higher than the current market price that the buyer agrees to pay in their signed contract to purchase the property.

Below are some interesting facts:

- There are many sellers in the market that do not know how to sell their homes or cannot sell their homes and they do not want to pay a huge commission to a realtor to sell it for them. Some have little equity or simply are not willing to discount their homes 70% of After Repair Value (ARV) to compete with banks. The After-Repair Value (or ARV) of a property is a critical number for Real Estate investors, as it helps determine the difference between the as-is price of the home and the value of the property after repairs. Understanding this calculation means understanding whether there is enough margin for the flip to be profitable.
- There are tons of buyers out there that cannot qualify for a mortgage to buy a house.

This is where wholesaling lease options comes into play.

The basic step to wholesaling lease options are:

- Find a motivated seller who is willing to sell their home under a lease option

- Get the property under an "Lease Option" contract
- Find a qualified tenant-buyer who has a good down payment and has a good chance to get a mortgage within 12 – 18 months.
- Sign the lease option paperwork with the tenant-buyer
- Assign the lease option documents back to the seller
- Keep the option consideration/deposit and give the seller the first month's rent (your profit)
- Help put the tenant in a credit repair program with a mortgage broker
- Deposit your money and move on

This option is good for potential buyers who cannot get a mortgage right away, because of credit problems, but are working on improving their credit and want to lease premium properties with the option of leasing to buy (or Rent to Own)

There are a few lease options I would like to discuss below:

- Sandwich Lease Options
- Cooperative Lease Options

Sandwich Lease Options

A Sandwich Lease Option is a technique that has been used for many years. When executed properly, you, the investor, will make money with the option fee, the backend fee, and a monthly cash flow. In a basic sandwich lease option, a person leases a property from the landlord and then sublets the property to a third person. The new tenant-buyer pays a higher fee which allows the original lessee to pay the rent to the landlord and to keep the difference, thus allowing them to make a small profit.

This mean that you get paid three (3) ways. Essentially, you lease a property with an option to buy, and in turn you rent it out to someone else, also granting them an option to buy.

You are in the middle of the entire business deal, which is how the name of this concept got the name "The Sandwich Lease Option".

And as you know the meat of any sandwich is in the middle. In my opinion, the meat is the most essential part of the sandwich. You do not go to a restaurant and order a white bread sandwich, or a multi grain sandwich. One typically orders the sandwich by the name of the meat that you would like, (i.e. hamburger, fish, chicken, etc.) and then you specify what type of bread you want your meat sandwich on.

Again, let me say that the meat is the best part of the sandwich lease option.

This is what we want to focus on… "the meat", which is you. How can we make the sandwich more profitable (by getting more meat in the middle)?

Below are the most essential components of this type of deal when negotiating with the seller and the potential buyer or lease holder.

- Down payment (Legally termed, the "Option Fee")
- Monthly fee (rent)
- Length of lease (how many years)

It is imperative to negotiate good terms with the seller of the property and have a solid contract in place with the seller and the lease/purchase of the property.

When is the sandwich lease option a good choice? When the seller has equity and will allow you to get part or all of it over time with your lease option terms.

Cooperative Lease Options

A cooperative lease option is like the sandwich lease option except the meat (the middle) is removed. Think of it as a sandwich without the meat.

This is where you purchase the property from the owner on a lease with an option to buy. then find a buyer who will pay you to step in your shoes. This is a wholesale deal. You sell your contract to a buyer.

How do you make your money in this type of deal?

Basically, you still find the seller and draw up a contract to lease their property with the option to buy included in it for the potential lessee.

In this scenario you only get paid one way and that is with the assignment of your option. You do not get the perpetual monthly income, but you get paid up front and once you have assigned the lease to a potential tenant-buyer, you are done with the deal. You get in and out quickly without any long-term commitment to monitor the activity of the lessee with the lessor.

It is important to look at this lease option strategy with the understanding that you are not finding a buyer for the seller, but that you are simply the principal interest in the contract and you have been given permission by the language in the contract to assign the contract between you and the seller to a tenant-buyer for a fee.

For example, you take a percentage of the tenant-buyers option fee as your assignment fee for wholesaling the lease option of the contract. This assignment fee can range anywhere from $2,500 to $10,000 (or even more) depending on what area of the country you are.

Steps

- You need to locate a seller with little or no equity that wants to lease their property to cover their mortgage payments until they can sell it free and clear.
    - Example: The seller wants $100,000 for the property; you assign a tenant-buyer for $103,000 and keep the $3,000 as your assignment fee. (all of this must be written in the option price section of the option to purchase contract)
    - Reach out to that homeowner to discuss a rent to own contract with a 3% to 5% down payment plus purchase price at the end of the lease option period. (you want to put this down payment in an escrow account with a title company)

- o You can also establish a relationship with a realtor that have hard to move properties that may be interested in this type of deal. You can offer them 10% of your assignment fee (make sure that you have an agreement that you can use their professional pictures of the property to market to potential lessees).
- o Look for people who cannot currently qualify for a mortgage, but have money and good jobs, who are trying to get their credit in good standing. Buyer must be a part of a credit repair program to show that they have good faith in being able to qualify for a mortgage.
  - Do background checks, credit checks, criminal checks, etc. on these potential tenants for lease to own contract.
- o These are some of the contracts you need to have in place.
  - Tenant – Buyer placement agreement
  - Option agreement
  - Sales agreement

  In both type of lease options, all repairs for the property are to be maintained by the potential buyer. There must be written language that states whether upgrades to the property can be made by the person leasing the property to buy.

- Once tenant is qualified to buy, the Sales Agreement will be executed. If you opted to remain in the deal utilizing the "Sandwich Lease Option", you will receive your agreed-to proceeds upon closing.

The cooperative lease option is good when the seller does not have much equity for you as an investor to tap into. There would be no need to wait until the tenant-buyer executes the purchase because there will be no extra meat on the bone for you, the investor.

Only choose the Sandwich Lease Option approach when there is a good amount of equity on the home available on the back end for you.

PART II

HOW TO MANAGE IT

Chapter 11

Avoiding Impulse Spending

Money and Emotion

It is hard to be dispassionate about money. Money can be a very emotionally topic especially when you are struggling with it. The best way to get the conversation started and develop a meaningful relationship with money. is to look at money from a practical standpoint.

Go over your debts, look closely at your assets, and determine what is the best thing for you to do with your time, money, and energy right now.

The point is simple: the only way to relieve yourself of the uncomfortable feeling of financial pressure is to act.

Let us evaluate your net worth. In order to get to a destination, you need to know where your starting point is.

Your net worth is your current financial state at this present moment.

The definition of net worth is the difference between what you own and what you owe. Assets – Liabilities = Net worth.

Let us start by listing everything that you currently own:

- Home
- Car

- Investments
- Savings
- Jewelry

Now, let us list what you owe (what do you have to pay others in order to retain your possessions):

- Mortgage
- Car Note
- Creditors
- Other Lenders

Your net worth represents where you are now financially. It is not a stagnant number, it changes as you earn more money, acquire additional assets and when you go into more debt and establish additional liabilities.

Tracking your net worth over time allows you to evaluate your progress, highlight your successes and identify areas requiring improvement.

Are you a spender or a saver? How do you go about making purchases in the moment? Do you do an emotional check before you slide that credit card? Are you motivated to spend by a "need" or "greed" (there is a big difference)?

Okay, "greed" may be a strong negative word, so let us soften the tone a bit and say "want". There is nothing wrong with "wants", but excessive wants will get you in trouble if you indulge in them often.

We must know the difference between a want and a need.

- **Needs** are the basic things of life.
- **Wants** are things that we would like, but not necessarily need to live – fur coats, designer handbags, high price electronic gadgets, etc.)

The key to saving is to understand your current situation. You need to identify all your incoming cash, how much you are spending on wants versus your needs.

Let's define Needs vs Wants:

Needs are the basic things of life, such as food, clothing, and shelter. Basically, anything that does not fit into these three categories is classified as "Wants".

Let's break it down further:

<u>Needs</u>

- **Food** – everyone needs food to function effectively in your body. Without food, the body will go into starvation mode and die.
- **Clothing** – I do not know about you, but the last time I checked, it is illegal to go out in public naked. Therefore, if you want to assimilate into society, you need to wear clothing that is appropriate for the environment.
- **Shelter** – Everyone needs someplace that they can lay their head at night, to replenish and prepare for the activities that we engage in to make a living.

<u>Wants</u>

Basically "wants" are anything that does not fall into the category of a "need". Below are some examples, but not all the things that I consider "wants"

- **Movies** - Going to the movies
- **Restaurants** - Going out to dinner and/or lunches excessively
- **Travel** - Going on vacations
- **Salons** - Going to salons (hair, nails, spas, etc.)

Unless you have an unlimited amount of money, it is in your best interest to understand the difference between needs and wants so that you can make better spending choices.

It can be challenging to accurately label a need from a want, and when those lines are blurred, they can impact your road to financial freedom.

Your needs should get top priority in your personal budget. Only after your needs have been met will you be able to allocate any discretionary income towards wants and savings.

These are a few questions that I challenge you to ask yourself before you make that next purchase. Is it a "want" or a "need"?

For us to maximize our savings and investing potential we must identify what is a "want" and what is a "need" and separate the two.

The things that we are spending money on that are "wants" are the potential opportunities to expand our wealth. Our wants are the things that we can put on a temporary hold to a future time in our life and utilize it to make our money work for us.

Most individuals will spend more money if they have more money to spend. As people advance in their careers and earn higher salaries, there tends to be a corresponding increase in spending, a phenomenon known as lifestyle inflation.

Lifestyle inflation refers to increasing one's spending when income goes up.

It tends to continue each time someone gets a raise, making it perpetually difficult to get out of debt, save for retirement, or meet big-picture financial goals. Lifestyle inflation is what causes people to get stuck in the rat race of working just to pay the bills (article by Will Kenton, Lifestyle inflation, May 0, 2018 – Investopedia.com).

This type of inflation typically occurs when one goes from being a student to a full-time employee. Despite getting by on truly little money as a student and skimping on everything from rent to groceries to nights out with friends, once we get that big paycheck, things that were once luxuries now become "necessities", and spending increases significantly. Sharing that two-bedroom apartment with three other roommates to keep housing and utility expenses down, suddenly becomes unacceptable, and you go out and lease a one-bedroom apartment in which you will live alone.

Lifestyle inflation causes us to live paycheck to paycheck, make the minimum payments on our credit cards, and not have any cash to fall back on when an unforeseen setback like a job loss or medical bill arises.

People tend to increase their spending with each pay raise or income increase, because they believe that additional goods and services, they purchase will make them happier in life. Often, they find out that the purchases if purchased on credit only makes life more stressful, not realizing that increasing their net worth by saving more, often increases their self-worth.

You can avoid the pitfalls of lifestyle inflation by learnings how to manage your spending and developing a savings habit that fits within your budget.

Avoiding lifestyle inflation can mean achieving financial independence at a younger age, having the financial ability to choose a dream job over a higher paying job and retiring early. How about that? Having the ability to choose a job that you love (with lessor pay) instead of one that you hate (higher pay because you are in debt).

This drives me to my next question:

What was your first introduction to money? Was it when you lost your first tooth, and the fictitious tooth fairy left a dollar under your pillow? Was it when your favorite uncle came to visit and always reached in his pocket to give you that shiny quarter when he stopped by?

Many of us have had various experiences that affect our relationship with money. Whether your first experience was positive or negative, we really need to understand the real purpose of money.

Money is simply a by-product of us tapping into our purpose. The skill set that we develop in life is what helps us to earn income.

Money is simply our life energy. We will our time for money. This means simply that every hour of the day that we are awake should be aimed at ways in which we can improve or enhance our experience on earth. Our time is valuable and should be used in the most productive way possible. Therefore, it is important that we manage this commodity called time more effectively.

The management of our money is where most of us blow it. We learn how to make it, but do not know how to manage it. There is a biblical quote that says that we should be fruitful and multiply and have dominion. Dominion (the power or right of governing and controlling, having authority —Webster's dictionary).

In the book "The Index Card" by Helaine Olen and Harold Pollack they talk about creating a flexible and realistic spending and savings plan. They go on to say that you cannot begin to save until you educate yourself about where and how you are spending your money.

You need to determine what day-to-day spending is necessary and unavoidable, identify what is a luxury, but helps you get through the day, and then what is excess. Only when we identify and confront our spending habits will we be able to avoid falling prey to spending traps.

Once we identify items that are considered luxury items, we will learn which items should be avoided on our journey to establishing financial independence. We next need to understand why we feel so compelled to buy these high price items. Don't get me wrong, there is nothing wrong with nice things, but we need to put it into perspective. Do we have adequate savings and assets that we own that can protect us if we fall upon bad times? Here is another question we should ask ourselves - Why do we buy expensive items?

Do we use money as a status symbol, to compete and compare with others? If this is what is driving us, then it is time for us to change the way we look at money. Do not get me wrong there is nothing wrong with buying expensive things that give us joy, but we should first make sure that we are financially secure to meet our day-to-day lifestyle expenses.

We need to understand that the purpose of money, which is a tool in our toolbox, is for us to have dominion over all the resources that we have at our disposal.

Just like any relationship that you want to develop and improve, we need to understand it, study it, and seek out knowledge on how to maximize the knowledge of how to earn it, spend it, save it and invest it.

I heard someone say once, that the only way that you can defeat an enemy is to study it and learn how they operate. Once you learn how your enemy operates, then you can develop a strategy to defeat it. Overspending is an enemy that we must defeat to gain our financial freedom.

If you are not where you want to be financially and are making good money, then you must recognize that the mismanagement of your money is the enemy of your maximizing your financial wealth. When we do not have dominion of our resources and make them work for us, we are under utilizing our personal finance capabilities.

We must have dominion over our resources. We must not just work for money, but we must learn how to make our money work for us. Our money should attract more money and wealth. This is how we have dominion.

Dominion is power. Power attracts opportunities, people, and money. Lack of power can repel opportunities, people, and money.

You cannot be your best you until you can live comfortably and worry free about your financial ability to control your resources.

Cutting back on spending can be extremely hard if you have not considered your motivation for buying things in the first place.

What is your reasoning/rationale for buying most of the things that you buy?

- A need to keep up with trends
- A need to reward yourself for hard work

- A need to impress your friends
- A need to make your kids feel that you are a cool parent

Now let us look at each of those reasons.

Trends - we will never be able to keep up with trends because the fashion and sales industries want you to constantly buy new items so that their profit margin is always growing. That which is in style today, will be out of style in the next sales cycle.

Reward for hard work – the best reward for hard work is seeing your savings account increase each pay period because of your ability to save.

Impressing your friends – if your friends are only impressed by you because of your materialistic possessions – you need a new set of friends.

Impressing your kids – trust me as a parent of two remarkably successful children, the things that impress your kids the most is the quality time that you spend with them.

If your spending habits are a result of unhealthy motivations, such as trying to fill an emotional need or "keeping up with the Jones", you will never have self-fulfillment.

Even, the best spending plan will not work if your spending is out of control for emotional and psychological reasons.

It is important to know that careless spending will not take away personal pain, and it could lead to serious financial problems.

Cutting back on spending can be extremely hard if you have not considered your motivation for buying things in the first place.

If you are really having trouble getting your spending under control, continue to ask yourself: Do I need it? If the answer is consistently "No", but you keep spending anyway, it could be time to investigate the root cause of your overspending.

Sometimes, all it takes is paying attention to your spending and watching what motivates you. In more serious cases, you may benefit from counseling or having an accountable buddy to run things by before your purchase items. It is so easy to use shopping as a crutch when you are sad or depressed. Try doing things that do not require money to pick up your spirits, like a good book, crossword puzzle or a nice movie on television.

Trust me it will take time to change your behavior, but if you make up your mind that you are tired of being broke, it will be a "no brainer". Once you do it for a couple of weeks, and see the difference in your bank account, the reward will be greater than the temptation to spend money on frivolous items.

Chapter 12

How are you spending the money that you earn?

Financial peace is not the acquisition of stuff. It is learning to live on less than you make, so you can give money back and have money to invest. You cannot win until you do this - Dave Ramsey

The first step in gaining your financial freedom is knowing where your dollar is going. You already know what is coming in, but do you really know what is going out? Are you in control of your out-going expenditures?

Taking care of your financial goals, requires planning and then setting goals. To set goals on saving, you need to know what you have available to save.

You do this by tracking your spending. Tracking your spending, as you go, can be difficult – you might forget to record some expenditures, or you might be temporarily tempted to avoid some expenditures because you know you are tracking them. The best indicator of what you are spending, is to go and look at three months of expenditures on your debit and credit cards and categorize them (i.e. food, clothing, rent, utilities, credit card payments, etc.).

This will show you a true picture of where your money is going. Have not you heard people say, I just do not know why I do not have any money? Where is my money going? By looking at three months of prior expenditures you will get a clear picture of where you have spent your money.

In looking at these expenditures, you will discover a lot of waste and unnecessary purchases (expensive lunches or dinners that you did not even enjoy). The facts are do you really need to spend $10 for lunch every day of the week? I am only talking to people that are trying to achieve a new level of financial independence.

This is when my husband and I had our wakeup call on our wasteful spending. Doing this exercise with our financial expenditures by looking at past purchases on our credit cards, really helped us to see all the waste that was occurring in our finances. I can't even begin to tell you how many times, I ordered lunch that I didn't even enjoy, when I could have gotten a salad or soup, or even brought leftovers from home that I would have enjoyed better. Once I realized how much I was blowing on lunches and dinners, I began to manage my food budget and realized more money remaining in my checking account each week.

I also looked at my entertainment and utilities expenses and realize that I was not even using all the cable channels that I was paying for.

In looking at your monthly expenditures and seeing what can be reduced or eliminated, you can quickly identify left over money in your checking account.

Once you identify these left-over monies, you will be able to put it to work for you, by saving and/or investing it.

The best thing to do with these monies is set priority goals such as:

- Debt-free goals
- Increased short term savings goals
- Retirement Savings goals

Are you surprised to see how much you spend on things that you really did not need to spend money on? Rest assured; you are not alone. You would be surprised at how much needless spending you will find when you look back at your historical spending habits. This is where you can clearly see "want" spending vs "need" spending.

You do not need to give up all spending on "wants", but when you are looking for money to further your financial goals, unnecessary spending is a way that many of us are leaking money without paying attention.

How do you compare to your peers in the country? When asked what household expense they would be willing to give up, 8 in 10 Americans ranked Internet service as a non-negotiable "must have" that they would not be willing to give up.

What would Americans be willing to give up:

- 66% Vacations
- 79% Gym and Fitness Membership
- 87% Gourmet foods
- 86% Facials and Spa treatments
- 85% Satellite Radio

Source: National Retail Federation

The things they were not willing to give up were internet service or smart phones.

Chapter 13

Plugging Spending Leaks

Okay, as with any goals that we set in life, you must have self-control and self-constraints, whether it be weight loss, acquiring an education, or building your financial empire.

Here are a few tips that you can use, to help reduce excess spending:

1. **Use cash instead of credit cards for your day-to-day spending:**

- Use cash for lunch
- Use cash for gasoline
- Use cash for miscellaneous spending

2. **Cut or reduce costly habits**

- Cut down on daily trips to the coffee shop
- Do not use the vending machine at work – bring your own snacks
- Bring in leftovers from dinner a few days a week for lunch
- Walk on your lunch hour – eliminate the gym membership

3. **Make a shopping list and stick to it**

- Grocery shopping – use list and stick to it
- Use coupons as often as you can

Examine your income and expenses to create a spending plan.

Below are some typical expenditures that the average person spend money on.

Phone Service – research alternate plans, could you save money by switching.

TV Entertainment

Subscriptions/memberships

Food

Extra Vehicles

Activities

Health Insurance

Car

Work clothes

Alternative transportation

PART III

HOW TO SAVE IT AND INVEST IT

Chapter 14

Develop a Savings Plan

We are all a victim of habits.

Unfortunately for most of us, we have no concept whatsoever of the psychology of habit, and, without being aware of the damaging fall out of this fault, most continue in the bad spending habits by overindulgence. Thus, resulting in us having extraordinarily little savings if any at all.

It does not matter how much money you make if you do not establish the systematic habit of saving you will never be financially independent.

If you get this basic principle of focusing on saving firmly in your head, then your road to financial freedom is well on its way.

Whether you already are saving, or you have not yet begun, your savings and spending plan begins where you are right now.

According to the Northwestern Mutual 2019 Planning and Progress Study, 22% of Americans have $5,000 or less saved for retirement, another 5% have less than $25,000 put away, and 15% have no retirement savings at all.

These are terrible statistics because there are so many benefits of having a healthy savings regimen. A lot of folks look at savings as something geared for the future, but did you know that "tomorrow" is the future.

Establishing a savings routine means allowing a break from the paycheck-to-paycheck cycle and establishing discipline in spending to be able to save for a big purchase. Also saving can help you to establish an emergency fund, so that you do not fall apart at a job loss, unexpected medical bill or having to take a leave of absence from work to take care of a sick family member. Having adequate savings creates a security blanket for unexpected emergencies. It relieves the stress factor when things pop up unexpectedly.

Saving sufficiently for the future – defined as either tomorrow or 30 years from now is crucial.

It is often said that it is never too late to start saving whether it be for a big bucket list expenditure (like vacation, purchasing a first home, paying for a wedding, etc.) or retirement. That may be true, but the sooner you start savings, the quicker you will get to your goal.

This is because of the power of compounding -what Albert Einstein called the "eighth wonder of the world".

Compounding interest means the reinvestment of earnings, and it is most successful over time. The longer earnings are reinvested, the greater value of the investment, and the larger the earnings will be.

Let us illustrate the importance of starting early using a retirement goal as an example.

Assume you want to save $1,000,000 by the time you turn 60. If you start saving when you are 20 years old, you will have to contribute approximately $655 a month a total of about $314,544 over 40 years at an investment rate of 5% to reach that goal. If you are waiting until you were 40 years old your contributions would climb to about $2,432 a month (that is almost 4 x the initial monthly contribution of $655). This shows that the earlier you start the less strain on your pocket. Sometimes it is difficult to try to catch up on saving for something that you could have started much earlier preparing for. Again, this is only an illustration that will be impacting by other factors in your lifestyle.

Now this little illustration seems easy, right, but it very few people that put it into practice. Why, because they have not made the necessary adjustments in their mind and lifestyle that enables them to make this paradigm shift.

Just think about it, when we wanted that new phone or that new pair of jeans, we saved up our money to buy that item. Our mind and actions were focused on what we needed to do to obtain this item. This focus and intensity are what we need to establish the discipline and habits to develop our savings plan for our financial independence.

It is always important to consider the big picture and develop and build habits that help you make better financial choices, leading to better financial health.

Millions of people, with the economic means to save, go through life with lack because they have yielded to destructive behavior that lends itself to no discipline. This prevents them from developing positive habits and a lifestyle that reaps success and prosperity.

The formation of a habit of savings is one of the greatest habits one can form. Forming this habit, not only conserves that which you earn in a systematic manner, but it also places you in the way of greater opportunity and gives you **the vision, the self-confidence, the imagination, the enthusiasm, the initiative and leadership** actually to increase your earning capacity. Through this Law of definite aim – geared toward developing the habit of savings, you are setting up in your mind, an accurate, definite description of that which you want, including the amount of money you intend to earn. Your subconscious mind takes over this picture which you have created and uses it as a blueprint, chart, or map by which to mold your thoughts and actions into practical plans. Once you develop this habit of savings, you will begin to demand prosperity, and you will begin to expect it, and begin to prepare yourself to receive this.

Therefore, as your earnings increase, your savings will increase in proportion. Once this habit of savings is formed, you will remove all limitations from your mind and begin your road to financial independence (an excerpt from Law of Success – Napoleon Hill).

It is important to know that what you spend your time and energy on the most will manifest itself in your life. If you focus on doing things that yield success and self-improvement, your life will benefit from the actions that evolve from your focus.

Personal finance rules of thumb for savings vary from individual to individual, that is why it's so important to partner with a professional financial planner that can help you map out the strategy that is best for you to achieve your financial goals.

How much should you save every month? Many sources recommend savings 20 percent of your income every month. According to the 50/30/20 rule, you should spend 50 percent of your income on the essential needs of life, food, clothing and shelter, 30 percent on discretionary spending and a minimum of 20 percent for savings.

The key to saving is to understand your current situation. You should know how much of your incoming cash is spent on your wants versus your needs.

Here is what I want you to do - Pay yourself first.

The secret of saving is to think of it as paying yourself first. It can be hard to resist spending today, until you realize that you are taking money away from the "future you". Pay yourself first means to set aside a predetermined amount of money for saving every time you are paid before using any of that money for spending.

If you wait to see what is left over from your daily spending habits, you are less likely to save. When you are on a real savings goal, for every increase in cost of living or raises you get, let it automatically go to your savings account. Learn how to live on what you are currently living on so that you can develop a habit of saving. This takes discipline and determination.

One common reason so many people get to the end of the month and wonder where all their money went is that they do not account for any extra expenditures.

Do not make this mistake, instead as I mentioned in the previous chapter on spending, look at your expenses and see if you are spending more or less than your projected amount that you set to spend when you set up your savings plan.

If your budget says that you should have money left over, and you do not then there is a problem. It is simply that you are spending it before you can save it. It is time to take a serious look at what you are spending.

Estimate what you want to save and have that amount automatically deducted from each paycheck.

If you are not good at budgeting and/or planning your money, take the money right out of your paycheck. base your living expenses off the net amount that you have left over.

All you need to do is figure out what percentage you can save off the top.

Determine your needs vs wants. Do you need to eat out for lunch every day? Do you need that specialty cup of coffee every day? Just think, by bringing you lunch a few days a week and making your coffee at home, or bringing your lunch and eating in the cafeteria at work, you can save $100's of dollars a month.

A good habit to use is the 30-day rule for all of your purchases that are not needs.

Instead of making an unplanned impulse purchase, delay that potential purchase for 30 days and deposit that money into your savings account. If you still want to buy that item after the 30-day period is up, then go for it. Otherwise, the money stays in your savings account.

When you realize how important your financial stewardess affects your ability to live a comfortable life in the future, you will start behaving different with your hard-earned money.

Chapter 15

Execute the Savings Plan

Now that we have developed a savings plan it is now time to execute the plan by putting it into action.

Create multiple savings goals: You should have more than one savings goal. Examples savings for emergencies, savings for investing, saving for retirement or children's education.

Here is an illustration of a simple savings plan.

For illustration purposes only:

Goal: I will save $5,000 in 12 months

The first thing you need to do is to do the math. If you are going to save $5,000 in 12 months divide $5,000 by 12 which equals $416 which is $420 rounded up.

Next, think about what you can do to make this $420.

- Side job
- Decrease spending
- Sell assets

Okay you can focus on one or more of the above, but the key is you have got to take actionable steps to achieve your savings goal.

Finally, to be successful in achieving your goal, you must first focus on what you need to do to get your thoughts and mind in alignment with your goal.

How do you save?

Sit down and look at all your incoming sources of cash (i.e., paycheck, side hustle jobs, royalties, tips from providing services to customers, etc.).

Next, look at what are your monthly expenditures (i.e., rent, food, transportation, etc.).

Look at what you are spending and determine what are your essential needs and what are arbitrary). Question all your expenditures. (i.e., look at how much you are spending on expensive lunches, designer clothes, gourmet coffees, cable subscriptions, movies etc.)

Then decide whether those expenditures are more important than the goal that you are saving for. This is where reality and discipline must kick in.

Do you want to continue with the no-value spending, or do you want to elevate your financial position by exactly increasing your net worth?

Once you realize the importance of savings and the role that it plays in your life, creating goals is the next step to stay on track. Only set goals that you know you can meet, otherwise they become unattainable goals and you set yourself up for failure and frustration.

You need to understand your cash flow: What it is, how it works and what your personal household expenditures looks like. Review your income and expenses and see where your spending habits lay. Be intentional about making changes to things you can, to make a positive impact on your financial position.

Automate your savings so that the money will be systematically pulled from your earnings and that the money has an assigned home for it to reside as it accumulates and earn interest. If you wait until the end of the month to save, the likelihood will be that there is not much left. Make it automatic and have money deposited straight out of your paycheck, or have a portion go into a savings account whenever you make a deposit.

More Tips for savings money:

- Save windfall income: any unexpected money, such as income tax refunds, bonuses at work, and monetary gifts from friends.
- Emptying loose change out your pocket or purse and put it in a jar and at the end of each week take it to the bank and deposit it.
- Try frugality – buy cheaper and off brand items to save money
- Break a habit – try giving up one expensive thing you do each week and put that money into savings (i.e., expensive dinners, gourmet coffees, night events)
- Save lunch money – According to a study by Forbes magazine, Americans on average spend $1,000 annually on going out to lunch. Bring your lunch to work and invest that $1,000 in yourself.
- Have a "buy nothing week".
- Compare costs of major items before purchasing anything. Do your due diligence, shop around before making major purchases.
- Use coupons – Coupons are a great way to reduce living expenses.

Sources: In Charge Debt Solutions and the Federal Trade Commission

With the average interest rate on U.S. savings accounts continuing to crawl along at approximately .06% since 2013, the traditional savings account is not the most attractive investment. However low interest rates are, this is still not a reason to not save. There are on-line banking options that pay a higher interest rate for your savings. But, regardless of whether your feel interest rates are too low to save, savings accounts serve important roles other than earning interest; they help you build up funds to cover both planned and unexpected expenses in the future. Do not save your money in your checking account, you need to have a separate bank account for your savings. It should not be co-mingled with your debit card checking account.

Chapter 16

Types of Savings Vehicles

While it may seem that opening a bank account for savings will require a lot of management and administrative work on your behalf, it will not. Automation is the best way to have your savings created and administered to your accounts. Money is automatically deducted from your paycheck and deposited into a savings account.

If you already have a checking account, opening a savings account at the same bank will allow you to set up free automatic transfers from checking to savings.

Below are some common savings vehicles:

- Basic Savings Account
- Online Savings Account
- Money Market Accounts
- Certificates of Deposit (CD's)

Basic Savings Account

This is the simplest form of saving. You deposit your money into an account, earn interest and withdraw funds when you need it. If your needs are simple, you can probably open a savings account a bank that you are currently using for your checking and payroll deposits.

On-line Savings Account

The best feature about on-line savings accounts is that you do not need a bank teller to take care of business transactions. On-line savings accounts are best for self-sufficient tech-savvy consumers. You cannot walk into a branch and get help from a teller – You do most of your banking online by yourself. However, managing your account is easy, and you can always call customer service for help. Because of the low administrative costs associated with on-line banking, interest rates are typically higher than a brick and mortar savings institution.

Money Market Accounts (MMA)

Money market accounts look and feel like savings accounts. The main difference is that you have easier access to your cash: You can usually write checks against the account, and you might even be able to spend those funds with a debit card.

However, as with any savings account, there are limits on how many times per month you can make withdrawals. Money market accounts often pay more than savings accounts, but they may also require larger deposits. They are a good option for emergency savings because you have access to your cash, but you still earn interest.

Certificates of deposit (CD's)

Certificate of deposits are also like savings accounts, but they usually pay more in interest. The tradeoff? You must lock your money up in a CD for a certain amount of time (6 months or 18 months for example). It is possible to withdraw funds early, but you will have to pay a penalty to withdraw before the maturity of the instrument. Certificates of deposit make sense for cash that you will not need any time soon.

Goal oriented savings:

These are accounts where spending is designated for things such as a new car, vacation, first home, and/or holiday gifts for loved ones.

Some banks may offer special accounts for these types of savings, but for sure many credit unions offer these types of accounts.

The main benefit of these types of accounts are psychological discipline for your goal. The interest rates may not be great, but you know the specific dollar amount you need to have accumulated in this type of goal-oriented savings, which allow you to see the fruit of your efforts when you reach your target goal.

Before you make any investment decision you must do your research and assess your tolerance for risk. You must not let fear motivate you, but the facts that you have before you. It is good to know that you have just as much right to financial success as the next person.

Once you learn from them, your past failures do not dictate your future success. Let no one put a label on you or put a period behind your name. Until the last breath in your body leaves, you will continually have chances to improve and expand your territory, based on decisions that you make.

Chapter 17

Protect Your Assets

Now that you have acquired new information on how you can invest into your future to earn interest and equity into investment portfolios and Real Estate, the most critical next step is protecting your assets both current and future.

Below are a few things you can do to protect your assets:

Increase your Liability Insurance

Many corporations have umbrella liability policies to protect the company in case a disgruntled or an injured client/employee decides to sue the company. Just think about it - you are a company. You are the CEO of your family. Each of us should view our assets and material possessions as if we are an enterprise. All of the hard work that you have put into your journey to get where you are today can all go up in smoke with just one lawsuit. Since we know that some people are professional litigators, and spend countless energy trying to find ways in which to enrich themselves at the expense of someone else, we must protect our assets.

Your first line of defense in litigation should be insurance. Call your insurance broker and increase your liability limits. Make sure your personal umbrella liability coverage is for an amount at least equal to your new net worth.

Consider keeping assets separate.

Depending on the state in which you live and the source of your windfall, if you deposit the money into a joint account with your spouse, this money could instantly become half theirs. For some, this is not an issue, but for others, this could pose a problem. For example, if you have children from a previous marriage and commingle an inheritance you receive with your new spouse, your children may get less than you expect when you die. This problem becomes even more damaging if you are contemplating a divorce

In the event of death, it could also cause problems. I know of an actual case of someone that lost their mother through death and they were the guardian of their mother, but because the mother had a joint account with the stepfather, the account could not be dissolved. The Stepfather died and no one had guardianship over him, so the money was untouchable without going through a lot of legal actions. I have not followed up with them to see if there were legal actions that they proceeded with. Until matters like that are resolved, the State in which the account was opened, usually keeps those funds in escrow where no one can obtain access. You should always do a living will to state clearly where your assets should go in case of death. Resolving these matters without a living will can take years.

Protect yourself from renters.

If you have rental property or expect to invest in rental property after doing your research and have the capital to invest, create a business entity such as an LLC or corporation to shield your other assets from a disgruntled tenant. By doing this, if your renter sues you for $5 million, they can attack the assets in the entity that holds the Real Estate, but the rest of your personal assets are protected.

Chapter 18

Dominion Over Debt

The real enemy of financial success is debt. Debt has ravaged this country like no other enemy has in the past 100 years. Do you realize that 100 years ago, there was no such thing as debt in America, that there was no such thing as a mortgage, and that 50 years ago there was no such thing as a credit card?

Umm, I wonder how our ancestors managed without such amenities.

Being debt free will allow you to build wealth and protect the debt that you have accumulated. You may not even realize how much your debt is hurting you until you pay it off.

So, stop making excuses and follow these six steps to get out of debt.

Make a List – this list should include all your debt, credit cards, and student loans. Include the interest rate for each debt. Rank the debt from the least to the greatest. This is the order in which you will pay off your debt (this is called the snowball affect). The snowball affect dictates that you pay off the smallest debt first then move to the next smallest, and so on.

Set a budget – once you develop this budget, stick to it. Eliminate spending on all things that we have identified in previous chapters as "wants". Look at other ways to spend less, such as lowering your cable bills and utilities, by using less. Aim to free up about $200 to $300 each month to put toward your debt.

Set up an Emergency savings fund – Rule of thumb 3 to 6 months of living expenses. Put this money into a savings account with easy access. This money is only to be used for emergencies when they arise, thus eliminating the need to use credit cards for these unexpected expenses. Keep in mind that an emergency is not replacing sofa or buying those designer shoes, it is for real emergencies, like appliances that break down, or a leaky roof.

Start paying down debt – now that your emergency fund is in place, you can start paying down your debt. Remember to use the snowball effect and pay down the lowest balance debt first, this helps to build momentum. Continue with this pattern, rolling the old payments into the next debt on your list, and you will eliminate your debt much more quickly. You can speed up the plan even more, by finding extra money to apply to your debts.

Stay focused – occasionally, you may need to find a little motivation or boost to keep your focused. Picking up extra odd jobs, getting a seasonal job during the holiday season or summer months can help you eliminate your debt much more quickly.

Focus on being debt free in the future – Once you have worked so hard to get out of debt, make a commitment to stay debt free.

Chapter 19

Conclusion

The truth of the matter is that one's wealth and financial health are very rarely on a straight upward trajectory. There is no guarantee that your income will be higher tomorrow, but you can guarantee that tomorrow will be easier if you start saving today and take control of your resources.

The more that you can save and invest today, the more freedom you will have tomorrow. As life's emergencies pop up, you will be able to handle them without going into a financial crisis.

I have realized through my journey that most of us have very little discipline in controlling our desires for spending money and very little experience with the concept of self-sacrifice (denying yourself a few conveniences of today to obtain a bigger prize on tomorrow, i.e., dieting, saving money, studying a discipline or a trade which takes a lot of our leisure time).

Once we understand the purpose and power of success and money, we will begin to shift the way we think about wealth and financial freedom. We were put on earth to be fruitful, multiply and have dominion over all our resources. The only way that we can do that is to have a plan and an intentional desire to do it.

It is when we begin to change the way that we think about a thing that the trajectory of the relationship with that thing will change. Between any two forces of nature there is a structure of hierarchy.

You do not need a six-figure job or family money to become financially independent. Instead, you need a plan, focus and discipline on how you spend, save and invest your money. Do not be afraid to get help with your plan if you need it. Studies show that a higher number of people who work with financial professionals end up achieving their goals as opposed to those with no guidance or counsel.

The most important tips that I can give you to help you achieve your goals are to be intentional, have a plan and be consumed with your purpose.

So, let me elaborate a little more on how important focus is on your road toward success and financial independence.

The primary driver of achieving the goals that we set is our unwavering will to succeed and the focus we apply to this will.

Focus brings our will into discipline. No successful person can achieve any goal in life without discipline.

This discipline is what I call "sacrificing" a little fun today to obtain an abundance of fun in the future. It is what it takes to strategically build a secure financial foundation.

These two things I know for sure:

- Focus is the tool that is necessary to achieve the goals of achieving financial independence. Without focus, it is impossible to achieve any goal(s) that we set.
- Focus is the key to becoming intentional about your future state, whether it be financial, spiritual, or physical.

We must eliminate all distractions and behaviors that are counterproductive to our purpose and our achievement of the goals that are conducive to our success.

You must understand that with focus you have the power to write the perfect ending to your story.

The perfect ending to any story is accomplishing the goals that we set. It does not mean that the journey is going to be ideal or perfect. It means that although the journey will have bumps in the road and setbacks along the way, if you stay focused on the goal and stay true to the plan – you will obtain the prize.

Always know your why, what, and your who. Why you were created, what your purpose in life is and knowledge of your target audience (your who). Once you know these things there is no stopping you from achieving your goals. Oftentimes people lose revenue sources because they have not conducted a market analysis of who their product will benefit. You must know who your target audience is so that you can accurately market to them.

We need to constantly firm up our goals and make sure that they continually line up with our values and that they are specific. We must be noticeably clear why we are doing what we are doing and what the outcome should look like (measurable).

Be definitive and on point. Have a check list for every action that you have identified that needs to take place. Every player must be accountable. No slacking allowed on your team. Even if it is a team of one. Absolutely no excuses are allowed. You must own every action and not blame anyone for failure. If you fail along the way on any action, look at it as opportunity to do better. But whatever you do keep it moving.

Stick to the checklist. Using the checklist helps you stay focused and on track. It keeps you focused on the plan.

Do not worry about outside chatter, nay-sayers and people who doubt your ability. You must be willing to lay your own bricks to build your own dream.

We must remember that the road to financial freedom is not a foot race, but a journey.

Let us continue to build our financial empire, one brick at a time.

Made in the USA
Columbia, SC
11 April 2021